D0230642

The Timetraveller's
Guide to . . .
ROMAN
LONDON

First published in 2004 by Watling St Publishing
The Glen
Southrop
Lechlade
Gloucestershire
GL7 3NY

Printed in Italy

ISBN 1-904153-06-2

24681097531

Design: Mackerel Limited
Illustrations: Mark Davis

www.tempus-publishing.com

ROMAN LONDON

Olivia Goodrich

WATLING STREET

Olivia Goodrich has been a Roman fan ever since primary school. Some of her most treasured possessions are five pieces of Roman mosaic, found while walking across a field in Italy. She lives in South London, has a garden but sadly no cat.

Special thanks go to her history teacher mother, long lost Roman playwright Kath Parsons and her new husband Gareth.

For all the children and teachers at Harbinger School.

CONTENTS

INTRODUCTION

Dear Mum,

They said it was at the end of the world and it really feels like it here. I miss home so much. It's so cold and wet, you wouldn't believe it. Please can you send me some thick socks and woolly pants as soon as possible otherwise I'll freeze to death on sentry duty.

I wish you could send me some of your stuffed figs too. The food is rubbish here. It doesn't taste of anything. They don't know what herbs are and they think olive oil is for greasing their chariot wheels.

Why did we Romans ever come to Britain? That's what I ask myself.

Your son,

Tremulus Frigidus

CHAPTER ONE

RAINY, WEEDY, WICKED OR WHY THE ROMANS DECIDED TO INVADE BRITAIN

Some people might be content with ruling more countries than you can count on both your hands but the Romans just didn't do things by halves. Julius Caesar had already tested the lie of the land in the summers of 55 BC and 54 BC, some say to boost his position in the popularity stakes. Needless to say, he made sure the Romans didn't hear the last of it. Those Britons were fierce, he said, with long hair, moustaches (and that was just the women!) and painted with woad, a kind of blue scary make-up for men (made from a plant with yellow flowers). He boasted he had made a brave venture, in the name of the Roman people.

So what was the big attraction for the Romans in cool, yes, and wet, Britannia? The Romans knew that there were natural resources to be had which they couldn't get their hands on elsewhere. They had already built up business contacts with merchants selling tin at Land's End (Belerium) in Cornwall and were importing it in the first century BC. We know that a place in Dorset (Hengistbury Head to be precise) was also visited by merchants from Gaul (the Roman name for France, in case you didn't know) in the early first century BC. Italian *amphorae* – funny long pottery jars with a pointed bottom – glass, metalwork and pottery from Gaul have all been found there.

The merchants must have kept their eyes open and ears to the muddy ground on their business trips to Britannia, sussing out the potential. They might have heard there was iron smelting going on in the Forest of Dean in Gloucestershire and in the Weald in Kent and Sussex. They must have seen the sheep and thought, 'cosy woollen rugs and clothing' – brrr, tunics and togas are not all they're cracked up to be when you get the furthest north the Romans had ever been. Anyway, what with rumours of gold, lead and goodness knows how much farmland (not to mention lovely boat loads of slaves), those merchants' stories were like music to Julius Caesar's ears.

For one reason or another, Julius Caesar went back to Rome and never returned to Britannia. More or less one hundred years went by before another Roman leader turned his attention to that mysterious place on the edge of the known world, as the Romans liked to call it. Claudius was now emperor. The harsh Romans mistook him for a bumbling old man just because he had a stammer and a limp. But really he was cleverer than he looked. His nephew, horse-mad Caligula, had been assassinated in AD 41 and Uncle Claudius is said to have been hiding behind the curtain…

It was now AD 43 and the honeymoon period was definitely over. Claudius needed to do something impressive and daring. Anything more successful than Julius Caesar himself was a plus point, so he decided to invade poor old unsuspecting Britannia. Well, actually, he sent his general Aulus Plautius along instead. Aulus Plautius took with him a formidable taskforce of 40,000 men which included infantry (on foot), cavalry (on horseback) and archers (and arrows). This time they were serious.

And, to cut a long story short, it worked! Aulus Plautius' battle despatch must have looked something like this:

Dear Great Emperor Claudius

Landed at Richborough, at the mouth of the River Thames.
Defeated Britons at the River Medway.
Got a bit wet trying to follow them across the marshes – we need to thank our Germanic soldiers for getting us out of that one.
Now camped near the Thames.
Awaiting further instructions.

Your loyal general, Aulus Plautius
PS. Don't forget to bring the elephants.

Without further ado, Claudius was on his way with, would you believe it, a troop of elephants. He marched with them into Colchester (Camulodunum) in Essex, the royal stronghold of Cunobelinus, king of the Catuvellauni. No wonder eleven kings surrendered to him, with a few elephants staring down at them. It was just a short trip, sixteen days in all. Claudius headed back, but his men didn't. The Romans were in charge this time.

Legend Has It…

The site of King's Cross Station was once known as 'Battle Bridge' for reasons long forgotten in the mists of time. But when labourers were digging up the ground in the nineteenth century to build the station a strange discovery was made. They unearthed some huge tusks probably belonging to mammoths, probably from the ice age and so probably absolutely nothing to do with Claudius and his invading army. But it would be exciting to think that they were the tusks of the elephants which Claudius brought with him to scare, impress, show off to the British peoples and that 'Battle Bridge' was named after the invasion battle.

Strictly speaking, there had been another planned invasion. Caligula had been ready and waiting to set sail at Boulogne in AD 40 but his army had not been so keen. He even sailed out alone to chivvy his troops along but they weren't having it. In the end he had to give up but not without the slightly loony idea, as the history writers report, of getting his men to fill their helmets with sea-shells and proclaim them as the 'spoils (trophies) of the Ocean'. I bet their hair needed a bit of a wash when they got back to Rome!

Caligula, which means 'little boot' as the army nicknamed him, lived life in the fast lane. He loved the lifestyle of a playboy prince, especially horseracing. He was even supposed to have made his favourite racehorse a consul. We can only begin to speculate what he planned to do on the eve of invasion:

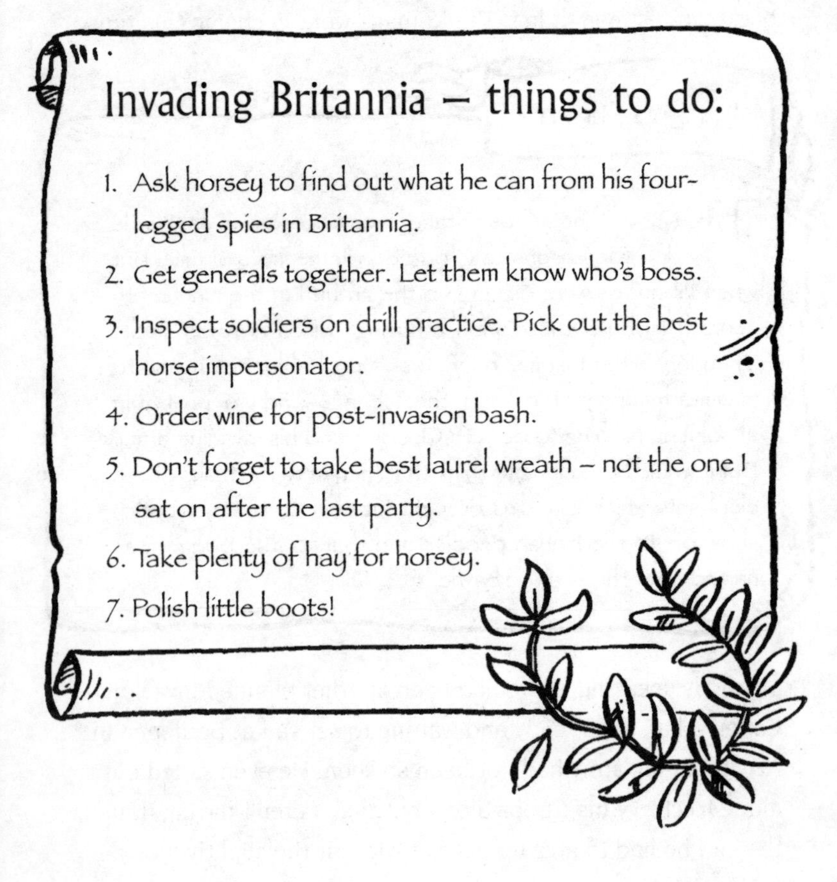

CHAPTER TWO

Roman Rulers or The Good, The Bad and The Insane

Caligula and Claudius were part of what was to be a long tradition of colourful characters in charge of the Roman Empire and it all started with Julius Caesar. He was the first dictator, king, tyrant, 'caesar', number one boss, call it what you will, of the Roman people. But his rise to the top was not a smooth one.

CURRICULUM VITAE

JULIUS CAESAR

Glorious army general and first to be one and only leader of the Roman people.

Main achievements to date:

60 BC: Elected consul – it's all downhill from now on!

59–49 BC: Hammered the Gauls into submission and invaded Britannia twice (just long enough to show them who's boss).

48 BC: Defeated dreadful old Pompey at battle of Pharsalus. Dictator, at last!

44 BC: 'Dictator for Life' – they can't get rid of me now! *

Motto: I came, I saw, I conquered.

Interests: Writing books about myself.

* Or can they?

Dictator for life was a step too far for his enemies. The ringleaders, Brutus and Cassius, murdered him a month later at a meeting of the Senate on 15 March, 44 BC. The fifteenth of March, May, July and October was called the 'ides' by the Romans. So if anyone ever looks mysteriously at you and says with a wink and a nod 'Beware the Ides of March', just agree with a wink and a nod 'cos you know what they're talking about. A shame no one ever said it to Caesar.

Caesar's successors also had lives which were far from dull. Here are just some of their career histories:

CURRICULUM VITAE

CAESAR AUGUSTUS

(formerly known as Octavian)

First and best emperor of the Roman people.

Highlights of sparkling career:

42–40 BC: Won, by overwhelming popular demand, control of Italy.

31BC: Defeated lovesick Anthony at Actium with landslide victory. Affected regime change in Egypt.

30 BC: Reunited Empire under my sole and just command - by the will of the gods!

27 BC: *Princeps* (first citizen) of the Roman people. They call me 'Augustus'.

27 BC – present: The golden years of 'New Rome'.

Manifesto: 'Glory, glory, glory!'

Interests: Me – I mean – the Roman people.

CURRICULUM VITAE

NERO

Emperor and first party animal of the Roman world.

My life in parties (the ones I can remember):

AD 54: Party after crowned as emperor – wow, what a rave up!

Party to celebrate murdering my bossy old mother.

Party every time I killed off an aristo. Who cares, they had really boring parties.

Life will be one big party once my golden pleasure palace The Domus Aurea is finished.

Skills and experience:

Excellent violinist. Even managed to carry on playing while Rome burnt.

Outstanding writer and composer. Always win first prize at every festival ever (perfect excuse for a party).

Interests:

Parties, the Theatre (it's in my blood).

Motto: Let's party!

Curriculum vitae

Hadrian

How I got where I am today:

Upbringing:

Born AD 74.

Brought up in Spain, born of jolly good Italian provincial stock.

Qualifications:

Bilingual in my beloved Greek.

Educated in philosophy, but man of many talents, especially architecture.

Greatest achievement:

AD 117 became a rather good emperor, though I say it myself. Some of the happiest years of Rome's history. Have tried to visit as much of the Empire as I can. Initiated heaven knows how many new building projects. For a start, have built a darned big wall across Britannia to keep out the beastly Picts. Will be remembered for years to come.

Favourite saying:

It's all Greek to me!

Interests:

Greece!

A rather splendid young chap called Antinous.

CHAPTER THREE

LONDINIUM WASN'T BUILT IN A DAY OR WHY THE ROMANS BUILT LONDON WHERE THEY DID.

Here are the main reasons why the Romans decided to build Londonium where they did:

A) There were two low, well-drained, gravelly hills, Ludgate Hill and Cornhill, on the north river bank which made a good building platform.

B) There was a constant supply of water from the river Fleet and the Walbrook stream.

C) The river Thames was wide and shallow (up to four metres lower at high tide than today) at this point. In some places it was shallow enough for a ford but in others it was deep enough for sea-going ships and had good enough banks for a bridge.

D) There were good jellied eels – or so they'd heard...

WHAT WAS HERE BEFORE LONDON?

We can be sure that there was no London before Londinium. The Romans were the first to take advantage of the site called 'plowonida' – the place where the river floods. Archaeologists have found no sign of occupation on the site of the future capital city before the Romans. The area was part of the Thames valley, a land clothed with patches of woodland and grassy clearings where the Iron Age people lived in scattered homesteads. They spent their time farming small pieces of land and hunting and fishing.

Wild West Town

Within the next ten years after the invasion, the first town rose up on the banks of the Thames. It was the sort of frontier town you might expect to see in the Wild West. Even then the town attracted people who thought the streets of London were paved with gold. They were wheeler dealer traders from other parts of the Roman Empire, many from nearby Gaul. They came to make their fortunes, selling their goods to the Roman soldiers and administrators. It would have been a bustling, noisy commercial centre. It was the first port of call for visitors from abroad travelling to the new province of Britannia. Roads led from Londinium to the far corners of the province.

The Walbrook Centre

A British Shopping Experience with Roman Style...

Browse the busy shop fronts selling a huge selection of local and imported goods: hand-crafted sandals – the latest in Roman design, exquisite glass tableware hand-blown in the workshops of Italy, fine quality brooches from the busy metalworkers' shops.

EXPLORE WHAT'S ON OFFER AT THE WOOLLEN MILL. CHOOSE SOME CLOTH FOR YOUR WINTER WARDROBE...CHECK OUT THE VERY LATEST IN ROMAN FORMAL WEAR: THE TOGA...IF YOU ARE OFF ON A TOUR OF DUTY, THEN MILITARY OUTFITTERS WILL CATER FOR ALL YOUR NEEDS.

STOP FOR A SNACK AT THE MANY HOT FOOD SHOPS SELLING FRESHLY BAKED BREAD, HOME-COOKED PIES AND VEGETABLE GRUEL SEASONED WITH CONTINENTAL HERBS....

AND IF YOU'RE THIRSTY...ENJOY A CUP OF SWEET SPICED WINE OR TRY A MUG OF THE LOCALLY BREWED BEER.

THE WALBROOK CENTRE – A TREAT IN STORE FOR YOU!

WHO BUILT IT?

If you wanted a town built in those days, then Roman builders were definitely the ones to choose. They were expert town planners, expert carpenters, not to mention expert road builders. They confidently carved Londinium out of the landscape, removing forests and top soil, flattening hills and filling in valleys. It was probably built by soldiers because of the way the roads were laid out in a type of grid (soldiers preferred marching in straight lines). The layout of the roads has lasted in some areas of London even to this day.

The first buildings were made of timber, with clay and timber walls (called wattle and daub) or mudbrick. The Roman builders had even invented house parts already put together. All that had to be done was assemble them on site. Let's hope they stood up to the wet and windy weather. These Mediterranean style houses were long strip buildings with narrow frontages facing onto the street, one storey high. The inhabitants lived and worked here. It was a workshop, home and shopfront rolled into one with a backyard for a few animals and vegetables.

How to Build a House in Five

The Barritus Housing Company

Manufacturer's notice: Please check none of the parts are missing before you start!

You should have: a set of squared, straight oak timbers for the base-plates, wall-plates and top-plates, vertical corner posts, intermediate studs, diagonal timber braces, tie beams, roof timbers, enough thatch for the roof, timber planking, a sack of plaster, wattle and daub and a supply of nails.

1: Location, Location, Location

Find a level, empty spot on the high street, near other workshops and a good water supply and drainage. Check out the neighbours before you begin!

2: The Frame

At this point get a friend or slave to help you. Slot together the timbers according to the diagram to make the basic frame, windows and roof. Strengthen with diagonal timber braces and tie beams.

3: THE WALLS

Insert horizontal bars between the stud timbers and weave around with the withies. Cover on both sides with daub, stamp with deep-set chevrons. When the daub is dry, render the patterned walls with plaster to a nice smooth finish.

4: THE WINDOWS AND DOOR

Construct shutters, sills and doors with any remaining timber planking. Keep front shop window as large as possible with wide sill for displaying goods.

5: THE FLOOR AND ROOF

Clear floor of excess debris. Cover with best quality clay soil and trample down until level. Apply the thatch, securing firmly to roof timbers – don't forget this is wet, windy Britannia!

WELCOME TO YOUR NEW HOME!

So if you were walking along the Via Decumana (the main high street of Londinium, a bit like Oxford Street) on your way to the sandal makers you might expect to hear a cock crowing in a back yard, the carpenter sawing a door frame, the splash of water mixed with other smelly, watery things going into the drain along the road; an olive oil seller shouting out his prices, the clip clop of a mule pulling a cart, not to mention the smell of freshly baked bread wafting over from the bakery and not so fresh odours from the dungheaps covered in hungry horseflies.

But three hundred years later Roman Londoners could tell a different story. By now Londinium had changed from a large and international port and administrative centre into a quieter, residential city. There were fewer people and buildings. But these were the town houses of the mega-rich landowners who also had villas in the countryside. And that's where the Spitalfields Roman comes in…

A Blast from the Past

Imagine the excitement and mystery when archaeologists excavating a Roman graveyard in the Spitalfields area of London on, would you believe it, the 'ides' of March in 1999 brought to light a stone sarcophagus (tomb) buried for nearly 1,700 years.

They didn't dare open the beautifully decorated lead coffin inside there and then. It had to be carefully transported to the special conditions of the Museum of London before that could happen. Questions started to fly:

The suspense was killing and it lasted for a whole month! Finally the agreed time for opening the coffin arrived: the evening of 14 April 1999.

Two film crews, three environmental health officers and seven Museum specialists gathered in a large plastic tent erected around the coffin and sealed up tight. No one knew what dangerous dust or diseases might escape! Then at 7.45 p.m. precisely, dressed in their white protective masks and overalls, the specialists tentatively slipped their gloved fingers beneath the lid and started to lift. It was the big moment everyone had been waiting for. There, revealed to the twentieth century world, was a perfectly preserved skeleton beneath a fine layer of wet silt. Meet the Spitalfields Roman!

A Woman of Substance

In fact, 10,000 Londoners came to meet this Roman stranger in the week that followed. With her head resting on a pillow of bay leaves, here was the miracle survival of the body of a young woman in her twenties, of great wealth and good health. How do we know? She was taller than average – 164cm (5ft 4ins) – and had good teeth. She had been buried in rich garments of silk and wool. The silk would have come all the way from China! In fact, her family were so wealthy that they had buried rare and expensive objects with their beloved daughter including jet hair accessories and an exquisite glass bottle used for holding scented oils.

And what about the question on everybody's lips – how did she die? Remember the skeleton was in perfect condition.

A) Did she die in childbirth?

B) Was she poisoned by the dirty water of Roman London?

C) Did she catch a nasty infectious disease?

Answer: C) *She probably died of some infectious disease that the Roman doctors were unable to cure. There are no visible causes of death left on her bones.*

CHAPTER FOUR

NEIGHBOURS FROM HELL

The people of Ancient Britain, before the Romans came along, were a truly mixed bag of peoples. They had arrived (and some of them left) at different times and for different reasons since the end of the Ice Age in about 8000 BC. That's a very long history of immigration! The last people to arrive before the Romans were the Belgae. They were a Celtic tribe from northern France and settled in south-eastern England.

The chief tribe in southern England when Claudius arrived with his army, was the Catuvellaunian tribe. Their capital became Camulodunum (modern-day Colchester) but Verulamium (St Albans) was also one of their strongholds. Cunobelinus was their king but, lucky for him, he did not live to see the Roman invasion. On his death, he divided his kingdom between his two sons Caratacus and Togodumnus.

Courageous Caratacus

The story of rebellious Caratacus could so easily have been a tragic one. At the time of the Roman invasion, he rallied support from anti-Roman forces in the region of Wales and fought the Romans beside the River Severn. The brave British were defeated and Caratacus fled north to the Queen of the Brigantians, Cartimandua. But little did he know, she was in league with the Romans and handed him over without further ado. Caratacus was taken to Rome to face certain death. But he made such an impression on Claudius that he was pardoned and saved from execution.

I Came, Iceni

The Iceni tribe inhabited the Norfolk area and were ruled by wealthy King Prasutagus at the time of the Roman invasion. Weak or canny, whatever historians think, Prasutagus made an agreement with the Romans which meant he could continue as king under certain conditions (keeping the Romans supplied with food and slaves, for instance).

There was peace and quiet for his lifetime, but when Prasutagus died in AD 60 things quickly changed. King Prasutagus, a diplomat to the last, had left his land and riches jointly to the Emperor and to his two daughters. But the procurator of Britannia (the governor's deputy in charge of finance) was the money-grabbing Catus Decianus. He gave the go-ahead for his heavies, the government officials, to move in and take not part but all of the possessions of Prasutagus. This they did and more besides.

They treated the Iceni nobles like slaves. What they did to Prasutagus's wife, the famous Boudicca, and her daughters is almost too terrible for words. They flogged Boudicca and raped her daughters. It was the cruellest treatment you can imagine. Flogging Boudicca was one of the silliest mistakes the Romans ever made.

THE JUPITER RUMBLER

BRITONS REVOLT!

TONIGHT OUR BRAVE ROMAN BOYS ARE ON THE POINT OF PUTTING A STOP TO A BLOODY REVOLT AMONG THE BARBARIC BRITISH.

The Iceni and Trinovantes led by Boudicca, wife and now widow of the Iceni warlord Prasutagus, have left a trail of destruction across southern England. Angered by a dispute over land, Boudicca has led a mindless attack on three Roman cities and viciously slaughtered the inhabitants.

OUR PROUDEST ACHIEVEMENTS IN FLAMES!

Our beautiful city of Camulodunum was the first in line of attack. Our honoured veterans have held out in a two-day siege. But now the magnificent temple dedicated to our Emperor Claudius has been flattened. Many have been massacred by the British mob. Members of the ninth legion have launched a brave assault but are now in retreat. Severe casualties have been inflicted on our forces.

BURNT TO THE GROUND!

That treacherous lioness, Boudicca has brought havoc to Londinium. Much of the city has burnt to the ground. Eyewitness accounts talk of terrible atrocities. Many too old to flee have lost their lives. Abandoned streets are left littered with the dead; hung, burnt and crucified. Latest accounts report that Verulamium has fallen.

DESERTER!

Procurator Catus Decianus has disappointed many in his attempts to quell the rebellion. Some say his actions have amounted to, in a word, betrayal. His slow reaction in sending troops to Camulodunum has cost many their lives. Many feel insulted that he could only muster two hundred poorly armed veterans to save their city. The procurator is not available for comment. Rumours suggest he has fled the country.

OUR GOVERNOR RETURNS!

But Governor Paullinus Suetonius is now in charge of the situation. With signs of exhaustion clearly showing from his successful Operation Druid in Anglesey, he has had to make some tough, on the spot decisions. Three of our finest cities are destroyed, two of them abandoned by our troops. Reports talk of an estimated 70,000 dead.

But tonight Paullinus is due to address our troops. Tomorrow the decisive battle of this vicious uprising will be fiercely fought out. Our boys are positioned at a point north of Verulamium, with woods and hills to the rear and with a river in front.

WARRIOR QUEEN

Intelligence reports suggest Boudicca is also rallying her 200,000 strong force. One eyewitness has even gained access to her camp and has sent this report:

'She was very tall and grim in appearance, with a piercing gaze and a harsh voice. She had a mass of very fair hair which she grew down to her hips, and wore a great gold torque and a multicoloured tunic folded round her, over which was a thick cloak fastened with a brooch.'

For more news from Britannia watch out for the late editions.

How It All Ended

Luckily two Roman historians tell us all about Boudicca's revolt and how she blazed a trail of blood through southern England. Tacitus wrote an almost eyewitness account as he was son-in-law of Agricola, one of the generals fighting in the campaign. Dio Cassius wrote long after the rebellion but used eyewitness accounts too.

The rebellion ended, by all accounts, with one of the bloodiest battles ever fought on English soil. The Romans were victorious. Although heavily outnumbered, their discipline and better weapons had won the day. The all-day battle claimed the lives of many more British than Romans. The Romans were so fired up with revenge, they killed everything in their path; women and children and old men too, even the oxen which had pulled the carts.

What about our heroine Boudicca? Tacitus relates that she poisoned herself, preferring the honourable way out. Dio Cassius reports that she fell sick and died. Whoever you care to believe, Queen Boudicca had almost changed the course of history. Just think, Queen Boudicca's great, great, great, great etc. granddaughter could be on the throne today! Her courageous uprising against a foreign power has never been forgotten. There is a bronze statue of her in her chariot just by the Houses of Parliament which shows how much the British people are proud of her fight for freedom.

The First Great Fire of London

Boudicca's attack on Londinium was devastating. The fire burnt the timber houses to the ground. Archaeologists have found deep down a layer of ash and burnt pottery in an area mainly east of the Walbrook stream. London, in those days, barely stretched a few kilometres from its centre at the river crossing near London Bridge. Just to prove how fierce a fire it was, archaeologists have done tests on pottery to see what temperature is needed before Roman pottery turns black and fuses. Results prove that the heat in the city centre must have been an incredible 1000 degrees Celsius or more (enough to fry an egg in an instant).

So if you happen to live today in the area where early Roman London was (or in Colchester and St Albans, for that matter) and you've got nothing to do in the summer holidays, then here's a project for you (and your dog, if you've got one). Try digging down about 4 metres and you are bound to discover a layer of ash and blackened bits of pottery. You might even make a more gruesome discovery, like a skull severed from its body. It would be just one of the many skulls archaeologists have found in the site of the Walbrook stream (now silted up) – the skulls of Boudicca's terror-stricken victims?

CHAPTER FIVE

Changing Towns

Once the province had recovered from brave Boudicca's bid for freedom, building began in earnest. A new governor and procurator were sent in to get Londinium and Britannia back on track. As the town prospered into a city, grandiose monumental public buildings made of stone began to spring up both north and south of the river.

A makeover of your town Roman-style, really meant serious changes. Agricola, governor of Britannia soon after Boudicca's revenge, was really enthusiastic about bringing the Roman look to the towns of his province. It was his way of bribing the British people into submission. This is what you would expect in your town after Agricola had finished with it:

THE LOW-DOWN ON LONDINIUM'S

THE CITY WALL

The wall was built in about AD 200.

It stretched around the city from the Tower of London to Blackfriars – more than three kilometres.

The main material was Kentish ragstone brought down the River Medway and up the Thames by water.

There were four main gates: Aldgate, Bishopsgate, Newgate and Ludgate.

The wall was roughly two and half metres thick and six metres high.

THE FORT

A fort was built in Kentish ragstone some time around AD 100 to the northwest of the town.

Soldiers working on the governor's staff used it as their barracks.

It was rectangular with rounded corner towers and four gates.

Top Property

The Governor's Palace

Also built some time around AD 100, the Governor's Palace contained offices and staterooms.

It stood under and beside modern-day Cannon Street Station.

The London Stone is thought to have belonged to its entrance

It had a spectacular garden terrace with a gigantic ornamental pool and would have been larger than the British Museum!

Roman Super Sleuths

London Bridge is Falling Down

Have you ever wondered what London would have been like without a bridge? Did you know the Romans were the first to build a permanent bridge across the Thames? The bridge must have been one of the first major construction projects the Romans undertook when they arrived. But where was it? Can you use your special super sleuth skills to work out where to look for the remains of the Roman bridge?

The Clues:

1. Two Roman roads converge at a point near the south bank of the river in Southwark.
2. On the north bank a Roman road leads down from the forum (more about that place later) and stops at the river, where Fish Street Hill is now.
3. A line of Roman coins were found dropped between these two points in the Thames in the 1830s when the river was dredged.
4. Archaeologists have also found two Roman shipwrecks further up the river away from the sea. How would they have got under a bridge?

What the Experts say...

The remains of a Roman bridge (it might not have been their first try) have been discovered a few metres further downstream from the present London Bridge, stretching from Fish Street Hill on the north bank to Southwark on the south bank. It was made of wood and held up by twenty supporting blocks across the river. The marshy land on the south bank must have tested even the

Romans' building skills. They had to put down logs as many as three layers deep on the waterlogged marshland.

But what about the shipwrecks? They think the bridge must have had a drawbridge in the middle like Tower Bridge to let the sailing ships go through.

What about before the bridge was built? The Romans probably crossed the river using a ferry or crossing at a shallow enough place to have a ford or lining up lots of boats in a row to make a pontoon bridge. This must have used up lots of boats because, during Roman times, the Thames was much wider than it is today. No wonder the Romans soon realized it would be much better, quicker, drier and safer to have a bridge!

Even though the bridge has been rebuilt many times, it has never moved far from the spot the Romans first chose.

CHAPTER SIX

THAT'S ENTERTAINMENT!

BATHTIME!

Bathtime Roman style was a bit more public than nowadays. As most people didn't have a place to bathe in their own houses it was necessary to go to the public baths for a scrub down. Keeping clean and staying fit was a Roman way of life. There were at least two public baths in Roman London in its heyday around AD 100 – one at Cheapside and the other at Huggin Hill. But as the population by then was about 20,000 there must have still been a lot of smelly people about!

But if you did get the chance to go, you had to make sure you planned your visit during daylight opening hours and had a small amount of money to pay the entrance fee. Baths were the same the Empire over so a trader from Syria might expect to find exactly the same layout in the London baths as he would in his home town.

Bathtime certainly wasn't a quick splash under the shower like we have today (that is asking a lot as it is). Roman Londoners would have set aside a good portion of the afternoon (when the water had had time to heat up) to spend at the baths which were a bit like Turkish baths you can go to today. On their first trip to the baths, Roman Londoners must have needed a guide to tell them what to do:

Wish You Were Wet?

Octavius Tufnellius Parkus explains the Seven Steps to Successful Bathing

1 – Step one, limber up in the exercise yard (palaestra) with a ball game or two.

2 – Then go to the changing room (apodyterium) and store your clothes away in the lockers provided.

3 – Head to the cold room (frigidarium) to shock your circulation into action.

4 – Next, thank goodness, is the warm room (tepidarium) with underfloor heating (hypocaust), especially welcome in wintry Britannia.

5 – Hotter and sweatier still is the next room, the caldarium. This is where it gets really steamy. Bathers use a strigil, a curved metal tool, to scrape off all the sweat and grime of the city. Then it is time for a dip in the hot-water bath to wash off all that yucky gunge!

6 – After that you go back through the different rooms, with a massage if you have the money, finishing with a bracing last dip in the cold plunge pool – ahhh!

7 – Time, then, for a drink and a snack, shellfish, or whatever you fancy.

A trip to the baths was not just a chance to invigorate your pores. It was also an occasion for socializing with friends and acquaintances. So as you lay outstretched having a massage with luxurious perfumes you could catch up on the gossip with your pal next door or strike up a deal with a business colleague as you scraped off the layers of sweat and dirt from your hairy armpits.

Men and women were meant to bathe separately but that didn't always happen in the smaller establishments. As you can imagine, there were a few bathtime scandals!

Amazing Amphitheatres

If you're an archaeologist you'll know that you don't find a Roman amphitheatre every day of the week (most days you don't find anything at all). But that is exactly what archaeologists did find in February 1988 when they discovered part of the amphitheatre of Roman London (five or six metres below today's street level) just near the Guildhall, London. It was in the north west of the Roman city near the fort and archaeologists think it may have been built soon after AD 70. Thousands of men and animals were probably slaughtered in the amphitheatre at Londinium during the two hundred years or so that it was in use as an arena for the games.

This first amphitheatre (which means 'theatre on both sides') on this site was made of wood. It was modernized around the time of Emperor Hadrian's visit (he was a great gladiator fan) in AD 122. The wall around the arena was now built in stone, just the right height to stop the wild animals jumping out and any scaredy-cat gladiators too. Archaeologists uncovered the eastern entrance into the arena and found a small room on either side of the passageway. These could have been restrooms for the gladiators perhaps with a shrine (a stone altar was found at Chester amphitheatre in such a room) for a last-minute prayer, something like this:

As in amphitheatres in other Roman provinces, if you went in the morning you would have seen gladiators (*bestiarii*) fighting against wild animals (boars, bears and wolves). At midday you would have been treated to some executions of criminals and later in the afternoon you could have seen gladiators (men and sometimes women) fighting each other.

If all that blood and guts didn't spoil your appetite you could go and get yourself a snack from a fast food stall outside or strike up a few business deals if you had the time. You could also do a fair bit of people-watching. If you were lucky you might spot a centurion off duty or even the governor of the province sitting in the dignitaries' box (*tribunalia*). Whoever was presenting the show (the editor) had the power to spare a gladiator or not. Thumbs down meant the gladiator who'd won could finish off his opponent.

Sportsnight

Desmonius Linius presents a round-up of today's events at the Games

The third and final day of the Games held in honour of the great Emperor Hadrian's visit was undoubtedly the most spectacular ever seen in Londinium. Rome's one and only Felix Fighting Troupe were the stars of the morning programme. Their fighting skill and range of technique were superb. The selection of brutal beasts really put their bravery to the test. But the final challenge came with the lions, especially shipped in from Africa for the occasion. What ferocity! What bloody carnage! How the crowd cheered as those criminals were torn to shreds!

At lunchtime we saw the execution of some wretched criminals. The crowds were baying for more. They loved it!

Then the afternoon kicked off with a parade of hippopotami. What a treat for the crowds! A hard act to follow but the gladiators were really on top form today. One after another clashed in mortal combat. Memorable was the fight starring Publius Ostorius of Pompeii. Again he lived to see another day, but it was thumbs down for his victim.

The animal hunt made a spectacular finish. The place was a riot of colour, animals from all corners of the Empire flooding the arena. It was a feast for the eyes and worthy of an Emperor.

But the real finale came with the torchlight display. What a dazzling light show under the night sky of Londinium! It really was a day to remember.

Gladiator shows seem to have been a popular Roman pastime in Britain, especially in the first hundred years or so after the invasion. Instead of posters of their gladiator-heroes, people had gladiator scenes on pots, walls and mosaics in their houses. Women as well as men enjoyed the shows. One rich Roman woman lost her pearl and gold earring at the amphitheatre in Londinium. It was found in the drains running underneath.

Quiz

1. The amphitheatre in Londinium was roughly the size of:
   A) Wembley football pitch
   B) Centre Court at Wimbledon
   C) A luxury apartment in Notting Hill Gate

2. The amphitheatre could hold:
   A) 6000 spectators
   B) One man and his dog
   C) 2000 spectators

3. The Romans built wooden drains underneath the arena to drain away:
   A) The blood
   B) The rain water
   C) The wine drunk by the spectators

4. The amphitheatre was also used for:
   A) Bathing
   B) Roman football
   C) The soldiers' drill practice

5. Incense was burnt at the opening and closing ceremonies:
   A) To take away the smell of the animal poo and human blood
   B) As part of a religious ceremony
   C) To create, like, a really, really mellow atmosphere, man

Answers:

1 – A) *Wembley football pitch*
2 – B) *6000 spectators*
3 – B) *The rain water*
4 – C) *The soldiers' drill practice*
5 – B) *As part of a religious ceremony*

What About the Theatre?

Some major towns had a theatre too. Colchester, Canterbury and St Albans all had theatres (the theatre at Canterbury held 7000 people, big enough for the whole town). No one has ever found a Roman theatre in London (so that's another thing to look out for when you're doing your summer holiday digging). But an important place like Londinium, the most prosperous capital in the Western provinces, really must have had one.

The theatre was the place for drama and also for religious festivals in honour of the gods. Some Roman plays had music and dancing, others were Roman versions of Greek plays and others were just plain bawdy comedy. Think of the worst slapstick comedy you can think of. Well, the Romans would have laughed like drains at it.

The actors and actresses wore masks on stage: a grinning mask for a comedy and a frowning mask for a tragedy. Of course, the real A-list celebrities of the stage were to be found performing in Rome. We know the name of only one actress in Britannia. Her name, Verecunda, was scratched on a pot found in Leicester along with her boyfriend's name, Lucius, a gladiator.

Some people think that the theatre didn't really catch on in Britannia (nor bathing), despite Agricola and his colleagues' efforts. Several important towns don't seem to have had a theatre and the theatre in Verulamium even became a rubbish dump before the end of the fourth century. Here are some of the possible reasons. Which do you think is the real one?

1. Roman plays were rubbish
2. It rained too much and it was too cold (Roman theatres were open air)
3. Roman comedy wasn't funny
4. The seats were too uncomfortable
5. They didn't sell popcorn in the interval
6. They couldn't see the actors' and actresses' faces
7. They didn't understand the Latin very well
8. No one really knows why

Answer: 8. *No one really knows why.* But *if* Roman *plays were like this one, then it's not surprising that* Britannia *gave a thumbs down to* Roman *theatres.*

Marcus Platipus Loses the Plot

A play in three acts by Octopus Maximus

Act 1, Scene III

(*In Marcus's front room. His wife Anthea and her friend Calpolia are lounging on couches, stuffing their faces and drinking wine.*)

Anthea: (*Taking a bite of something.*) You know these swan pies are not up to our cook's usual standard. Where are they getting their swans from these days? This tastes like the smell of one of the dodgier stretches of the Thames.

Calpolia: It's this wretched climate if you ask me. The meat is always so soggy, just like old sandals that have been left out in the rain...

Anthea: Rain...the never-ending rain!...

(*They exchange despairing looks.*)

Calpolia: Chuck us the amphora, Anth. Let's drown our sorrows and make a toast to the motherland.

(*Calpolia fills their glasses from the amphora and they toast.*)

Anthea: Up with olive groves and designer togas!

Calpolia: Down with beer and overcooked vegetables!

(*Pause while they drink.*)

Anthea: Have I told you how Marcus has been being a bit of a pain since he was elected onto the Provincial Council?

Calpolia: No…

Anthea: Well he thinks he's so blimmin' important, by Minerva! Swaggering around the house pretending to make speeches starting 'Fellow citizens of Londinium'. His head has swollen to the size of an amphith…

Calpolia: Keep your voice down, I can hear someone – it might be him.

Anthea: (*In an undertone*) I know what…

(*She removes a lump of swan from her half-eaten pie and wipes it over the floor. Marcus enters.*)

Marcus: (*Striding forward purposefully*) Fellow citizens of Lond–aaah!

(*At this point he slips on the swan grease, falls over and is knocked out. The ladies laugh themselves silly.*)

Anthea: Let's bundle him up and have him thrown to the wolves at the next games.

Calpolia: Oooh Anth, you are wicked!

(*They exit, Anthea dragging Marcus by the hair.*)

CHAPTER SEVEN

Hotline to the Gods

Contacting the gods to predict the future or influence future events was a part of daily life for Roman Londoners. They had a whole variety to choose from. It was really a matter of wealth and how desperate you were to get what you wanted. Offerings ranged from paying for a stone altar, sacrificing an animal or bird or a small object.

A range of sacred objects have been found in Roman London, especially in the cemeteries, the Walbrook Stream and the River Thames. They include Venus figurines, amulets (a piece of jewellery worn as a charm), a statue of the British hunter-god and a plaque of the three Celtic mother-goddesses.

Roman Super Sleuths

The Traditional Roman Gods

The ancient Roman gods, the old favourites of the more traditional times, were certainly part of formal worship in Londinium.

The Clues:

1. Fragments of a monumental arch showing gods like Mars and Mercury found at Blackfriars in 1975 and reused in a defensive wall along the riverbank.

2. Parts of a 'Screen of Gods' showing deities like Vulcan and Minerva found at Blackfriars.

What the Experts say...

The arch could have been part of a religious complex or it could have spanned a main street in Londinium. The 'Screen of Gods' was a wall of gods, the sort usually found within temple buildings.

Who's Who?

Top Ten Favourite Gods and Goddesses:

1. Jupiter:

Main job: Boss of Olympus

Famous for: Thunder and seducing unsuspecting maidens

Greek counterpart: Zeus

2. Juno:

Main job: Queen of Olympus, sister and husband of Jupiter

Famous for: Protecting women and marriage, standing up to her husband

Greek counterpart: Hera

3. Mars

Main job: Scary god of war

Famous for: The month of March, the red planet and a chocolate bar are all named after him

Greek counterpart: Ares

4. Minerva

Main job: Brainy goddess of wisdom, arts and crafts of peace and war

Famous for: Wearing armour even when she was born full-grown from the head of Jupiter

Greek counterpart: Athena

5. Mercury

Main job: Messenger and general dogs body of the gods

Famous for: His fancy helmet and shoes with wings

Greek counterpart: Hermes

6. Neptune

Main job: God of the sea

Famous for: His scraggly, salty beard and pointy trident

Greek counterpart: Poseidon

7. Diana

Main job: Goddess of the moon and hunting

Famous for: Her fast legs and bow and quiver

Greek counterpart: Artemis

8. Venus

Main job: The goddess of love and beauty

Famous for: Her stunning good looks, winning the golden apple in the Judgement of Paris, being born from the foam of the sea

Greek counterpart: Aphrodite

9. Apollo

Main job: God of the sun, music and medicine

Famous for: His flashy chariot which he rode across the sky

Greek counterpart: Apollo

10. Saturn

Main job: God of growth and farming

Famous for: Saturday, the planet Saturn and the Roman version of Christmas, the Saturnalia, are all named after him

Greek counterpart: Cronus

CLARINUS RAYNOX SOLVES YOUR PROBLEMS

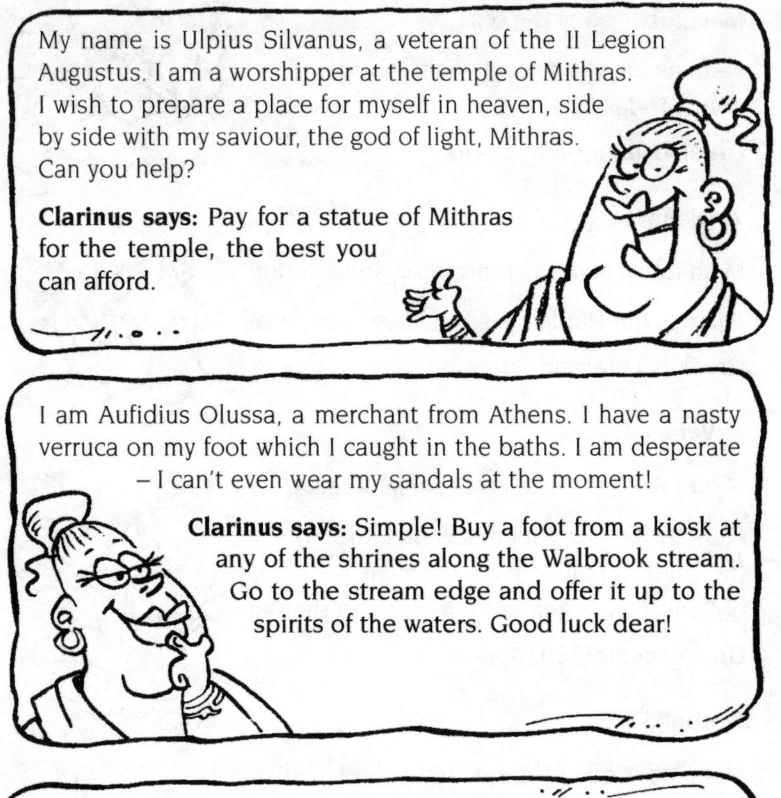

I am Claudia Martina, wife of Anencletus a slave of the Provincial Council, and I wish for a child. I will do anything to bring this about!

Clarinus says: Make a dedication to the mother-goddesses, a figurine will do. You will please the goddesses even more if you can afford a plaque from tin or a sculpture from stone. Have it put up in the temple in the east of the city.

I am Gaius Suetonius Paullinus, Governor of the province of Britannia. I am shortly to embark on a fierce battle with the dreaded Druids in Anglesey. I am desperate to know the outcome.

Clairinus says: Go to the temple of Mars and sacrifice a goat, the most expensive you can afford. Take it to the haruspex (that means 'gut gazer') to examine the liver. May the god of war have mercy on you and your brave, brave soldiers.

Roman City Super Sleuths

Emperor Worship

The Romans didn't just worship a whole range of gods, they even worshipped their own emperors! All the evidence suggests that they brought their brand of ruler worship to Londinium.

The Clues:

1. In Colchester there are remains of an extensive temple mentioned by the Roman historian Tacitus.
2. Remains of a small classical Greek-style temple have been found at what would have been the heart of Londinium.

What the Experts say...

Both temples were almost certainly dedicated to the Imperial House. That means it was the place to go and show your face and make an offering if you wanted to suck up to the Romans. Everything in it would have been to do with the emperor: statues, altars, inscriptions, you name it.

In the early days after the Roman invasion when Colchester was the principal town, the temple built there to the emperor Claudius was really something special. It was a magnificent marble-clad building, one of the most ambitious public buildings north of the Alps. It could be seen for miles around. But, you guessed it, nothing much remains of it today. After a temple it became a fortification, then a Norman castle and now the Colchester museum stands on its foundations.

When Londinium started to flourish as capital of the province, then the clues point to a temple to the Imperial cult being built there too. It would have been part of the forum complex.

Mind Your Language

Cursing comes near the top of the list of 'Things we must try not to do at school'. But cursing Roman-style was not only allowed, it was a serious business. It wasn't just a matter of saying a forbidden swear word, it even involved the gods.

Here's a real curse, found written on a scrap of lead near Moorgate in 1934. It was nailed face down with the magical number of seven nails probably at a wooden shrine by the Walbrook Stream.

'I curse Tretia Martia and her life and mind and memory and liver and lungs, mixed up together, and her words, thoughts and memory; thus may she be unable to speak what things are concealed...'

Poor old Tretia Martia. I wonder what happened to her. I bet you can think up a curse about a nasty teacher. What would it say? Here are some instructions to help you:

Beginners Guide to Cursing

1. If you want the gods' help to seek revenge or solve a crime, then a curse is the ideal solution.
2. Write your curse on a metal sheet made of pewter or lead.
3. First write the name of the god or goddess who you want help from.
4. Then write down the name of the person you are cursing and the reason why.
5. Then write down the most evil thing you can think of which you want to happen to them.
6. When you've finished, use your lucky number of nails to nail it to your favourite tree in the playground.

It might look something like this:

To Minerva, the goddess of wisdom: I curse my nasty teacher and her cat and her garden and everything she tries to grow there because she makes us do PE in the rain every week.

May she choke on her packed lunch in front of all the teachers in the staff room!

The Dreaded Druids

The Romans usually had an attitude of 'live and let live' when it came to foreign gods but not where the dreaded Druids were concerned. Whether it was true or not, they thought the Druids were troublemakers. They were powerful magicians who stirred up resistance to the Romans amongst the Britons and they practised savage human sacrifice. This is what Diodorus Siculus, a Roman historian, had to say about the druids in Gaul and other Celtic priests:

Now that's a gruesome and blood curdling way to tell fortunes! It's a shame they didn't have tea leaves in Roman times or a chance to visit Gypsy Rose Lee at the end of the pier.

A TASTE OF THE ORIENT

But it was boring always worshipping the same old gods. Roman Londoners began to look for something a bit more exciting. They thought the cults brought from the East by merchants and soldiers were guaranteed to spice up their spiritual lives.

AWFUL ISIS

No temple has been found in Londinium dedicated to the Egyptian god Isis but have a look at these two clues and see what you think.

The Clues:

1. A wine flagon (a type of jug) found with an inscription 'At London, at the Temple of Isis'
2. An altar was unearthed which commemorates the rebuilding of a temple (probably) of Isis by the provincial governor

What the Experts say...

The worship of Egyptian Isis went on in lots of other parts of the Roman Empire. So the chances are it must have gone on in London. If you'd stepped inside that temple, you would have been greeted by the sight of priests with shaven heads, mourning and wailing. Why, you may ask? If you think the arguments you have with your family are bad, well the ugly quarrels in Isis's family were even worse.

Unfortunately, Osiris was both the brother and lover of the Eyptian goddess Isis. This upset Set who was the other brother of Isis. So he decided to kill Osiris. But Isis managed to give life to the scattered limbs of Osiris. However, she herself came to a sticky end when her son, Horus, turned on his mother and cut off her head because she wouldn't let him kill Set. Got that?

So what was the attraction in all of this murder and matricide (killing your mum)? Well, the worshippers of Isis believed she could give life after death to them, just as she had done to Osiris.

Cruel Cybele

The next set of clues are to do with the Great Mother Goddess from Turkey called Cybele.

The Clues:

1. A pair of bronze forceps (sharp pincers) 29cm long, decorated with the heads of Atys and Cybele were fished out of the Thames at London Bridge.
2. A stone statue possibly of Atys has been found.
3. A small statue said to be of Atys has also been recovered.

What the Experts say...

Cybele had a tragic tale of love too. She fell for a young man called Atys but, to cut a long story short, he did not fall in love with her. So Cybele took revenge by driving young Atys to madness. In fact, he became so mad that he castrated himself (chopped his own dangly bits off!) and bled to death. To be a priest in this mystic cult, you had to, wait for it, copy Atys and castrate yourself as part of your initiation – ouch! Go to the British Museum and you will see the pair of bronze forceps found in the Thames and probably used for this very purpose.

Mighty Mithras

The guesswork is a little easier when it comes to the mystery cult of Mithras. You can even go and see the temple for yourself. It's still visible below the streets of London.

HOLD THE FRONT PAGE!

The discovery of the temple of the Persian god Mithras in London in 1954, on a bomb site near the Mansion House and by the Walbrook stream, was the greatest achievement of London archaeologist W.F. Grimes. On 18 September, what was supposed to be the last day of the dig, archaeologists unearthed the marble head of Mithras. They went on to uncover other beautifully sculptured heads of deities which once adorned the temple. The excavation caught the imagination of the London people. Tens of thousands of people queued up to see the temple. The queue on the last day was said to stretch almost two kilometres long and hundreds were turned away when darkness fell.

The Clues:

Found at the site were:

1. The foundations of an early church-shaped building
2. A marble head of Mithras
3. The heads of other gods including Minerva, the wine god Bacchus and Serapis, Egyptian God of the Underworld
4. Remains of animal sacrifice
5. Candlesticks
6. An ornate silver box with an infuser inside

What the Experts say...

The cult of Mithras drew in the crowds in Roman times too. It was Christianity's strongest rival in the Roman world (sadly, if you were a woman you couldn't join). It was a favourite with soldiers, officials and merchants. If you joined, you had to follow its high moral code. That means you had to behave yourself, which didn't really go with religion in Roman times. You had to be (or try to be) honest, pure and full of courage. In return, you had the promise of life after death.

Yet More Mystery

Apart from finding remains of animal sacrifice, candlesticks and a marble head of Mithras that had been burnt, archaeologists found an ornate silver box with an infuser inside. It was discovered in a secret hiding place in the wall. It had remarkable decoration on it, including mythical griffins trying to tear open boxes, a bit like coffins, with men in some of them. Perhaps it was used to make the magical herbal infusion which worshippers were known to drink as part of the ceremonies. It would be nice to think so but no one knows for sure.

ROMAN SUPER SLEUTHS

CAPITAL CHRISTIANS

There is very little trace left behind of the Christian community in late Roman London. Have a look and make up your own mind:

The clues:

1. Many of the precious objects in the temple of Mithras were found buried hurriedly under the floor and others smashed and scattered far and wide. Chief suspects? – the cruel Christians!
2. A handful of objects were found with a Christian symbol on them. This symbol was the first two Greek letters of the name of Christ, an X and an R (Chi-Rho).
3. Restitutus, Bishop of London, went along with two other British bishops to an important international conference of church leaders in Arles in Gaul only two years after Constantine's conversion in AD 312.

WHAT THE EXPERTS SAY...

The most famous religion to come from the east was Christianity. By the third century (the 200s) Christianity had spread throughout the empire. But it was not safe to be a Christian. The emperors tried to stamp it out and Christians were treated in all sorts of bloodthirsty ways. There are known to be three Christians who were put to death in Britain; Julius and Aaron were put to death in Caerleon in South Wales, and Alban had his head chopped off outside Verulamium. He is the most famous, known as the first British saint and martyr, and St Albans is named after him.

But this didn't stop the courageous Christians. Of course, it helped when the emperor Constantine converted to Christianity in AD 312. This gave the all-clear for Christians to come out of hiding. But the Christians of Roman London were none too tolerant themselves when it came to their chief rival: Mithraism. They were, in some ways, too similar for comfort.

Similarities

1. They both demanded high ideals.
2. They both had a sacred meal during a secret ceremony.
3. They both ate sacred flesh (or something that stood for this) and drank a special drink.

Differences

1. Anyone could be a Christian. Only men could follow Mithras.
2. Christians believed in one God. Mithraism allowed followers to worship other gods apart from Mithras.

LEGEND HAS IT...

SOME PEOPLE BELIEVE THAT THE CHURCH OF ST PETER-UPON-CORNHILL IS VERY ANCIENT INDEED. THEY SAY THAT IT WAS FOUNDED IN AD 179, RIGHT BACK IN ROMAN TIMES WHEN IT MUST HAVE BEEN KEPT SECRET TO SURVIVE AT FIRST. IT CELEBRATED ITS 1800TH BIRTHDAY IN 1979. EVEN YOUR GRANNY ISN'T QUITE THAT OLD!

CHAPTER EIGHT

Lifestyles of the Rich and Roman

Never Prosaic Mosaics

'If you've got it, flaunt it' was the motto for the rich and wealthy of Roman London. They were experts at showing off their riches. The biggest, brashest way was to pay for something for the public like the shows at the amphitheatre or a temple.

Roman Londoners keen to climb the social ladder also lavished money on their houses. After a flamboyant new wall painting or a state of the art central heating system, chief among the status symbols were mosaics. They took a long time to make and were expensive. But if you wanted to make friends and influence them, then they were the latest thing to have.

Of course, the best place to have a mosaic was in the room where visitors could marvel at it the most. The dining room, for instance, had maximum show-off potential. Just think how practical it was too. It didn't matter how many crumbs and other not so tasty morsels fell on the mosaic floor. The slaves only needed to give it a sweep and a wash and it would be as good as new (no vacuum cleaners in Roman times).

But apart from the practical side, mosaics (and wall paintings too) added a splash of colour to the dullest of dining rooms. Remember Romans didn't have jazzy curtains or swirly carpets. With the help of cubes cut from pottery, different coloured stones and sometimes blue glass, Roman Londoners created bold geometric patterns and larger than life scenes of people and animals. Scenes showing myths were old favourites. There are two famous mosaics from Londinium which show the god of wine, Bacchus.

Another impressive mosaic was found in Victorian times when builders were constructing Queen Victoria Street near the Mansion House. It's called the Bucklersbury mosaic and its discovery caused such a sensation that 50,000 people flocked to see it over three days. You can still see it in the Museum of London.

Grander still were the mosaics found in the country villas of seriously rich landowners. Fine villas and even finer mosaics sprung up in the Romanized country areas. The palatial villa at Woodchester in Gloucestershire has the largest known mosaic floor in north-west Europe!

What? No Mosaics?

Sadly we can only feast our eyes on a few remaining mosaics. Many Roman London mosaics have been bulldozed away without trace, some before the very eyes of the helpless archaeologists. Even Roman Londoners removed mosaics when they were abandoning the city at the end of Roman times.

Some could not be bothered to do even this (or didn't have the cash) so the mosaics fell into disrepair. The Christians, too, might have had a hand in mosaic mutilation. They liked to destroy anything which showed the gods and goddesses of pagan (the Christian name for anything that wasn't Christian) belief.

Hot Housing

Mosaics had never been seen before on the shores of Britannia but nor had the fancy central heating which Romans invented. It really must have been a very attractive side of Roman rule for the shivering elite in wet and draughty Britannia. This underfloor heating was known as hypocaust. No more smelly and smoky fires. The Romans did it a cleaner way.

Hot air flowed under the floors (raised on brick columns) and up the walls in channels built of hollow tiles. The air was heated in a furnace where charcoal was burned. This is how the air was heated for the tepidarium and the caldarium at the Roman baths, just like the bathhouses found in Roman London. This must have been a vote winner. Chilblains were out; Romans and their heating were in!

But the wealthy fat cat landowners of later Roman Britain fancied the idea of heating in their own villas. This is what you can see if you visit a once magnificent Roman villa at Chedworth in Gloucestershire. The villa has a hypocaust (and a fine mosaic) from the villa's very own private baths.

CHANGING VILLAS

WITH LAURENTIUS L. BOWENUS, FAMOUS INTERIOR DESIGNER FROM GREECE.

(Opening titles fade. Cut to Laurentius L. Bowenus, luxuriating on a sumptuous couch. He gives a flick of his long, flowing hair and faces the camera.)

Laurentius (*smiling*): I'm thinking mosaics, opulent mosaics, mosaics with chintz borders, bowls of overflowing fruit, cherubs eating grapes. (*Laurentius throws his head back, opens mouth and drops, with a flourish, some grapes into his gob. At this moment Handious Andius, his Celtic slave enters, balancing a water feature on his head.*)

Laurentius (***startled by Andius, begins choking and turning red in the face***): We…eerg…nnnne (***coughing and gurgling, he finally spits out the grapes***). Weeee… (***regaining his composure***) need wall paintings, rich colours, purples, mauves and lilacs.

Andius (***drops the water feature with a crash***): Bish, bash bosh, eh boss?

Laurentius (***raising left eyebrow***): I ask you, how am I supposed to work in this miserable backwater? Lindius Barkus got Fishbourne, for Jupiter's sake! **(*Sighs*)** Okay, Andius, let's go with the idea about the new door here into the garden, fountains, rose beds, sea view…

Chips Are Off

Potatoes hadn't reached Britain in Roman times. No chips or crisps, then, or chocolate, for that matter. Instead, Roman Londoners ate the meat, fish, poultry, grains, vegetables, fruit and bread they had always eaten with some exciting new exotic foods imported by the Romans (if they could afford it). Olive oil, new herbs (mustard, mint, coriander, dill and fennel), olives, dried figs and garum (a spicy, salty fish sauce made from fish guts) were all introduced by the Romans. Honey (used instead of sugar) was popular in Roman recipes, even in the same recipe as sour garum!

If you think school dinners are like the contents of your neighbour's compost heap, then see if you would have eaten any of these Roman delicacies:

- Snails fattened on milk until they were too big to squeeze back into their shells
- Battery dormice: dormice fattened on nuts in special earthenware jars
- Pigeons immobilized by having their wings clipped or legs broken, then fattened
- Chicken cooked in a variety of ways – in one recipe you had to drown a live chicken in red wine

Dress to Impress

There is barely any evidence from Roman London to tell us what Roman Londoners wore. There are only a few well-preserved leather sandals and even an acrobat's leather bikini. Why do you think this is?

A) Roman Londoners didn't wear clothes.

B) Roman Londoners took all their clothes with them when they left.

C) Cloth rots away easily in damp conditions, only leather survives well.

Answer: C) *Leather items have been found in damp places like the Walbrook stream and at the bottom of Roman wells.*

But statues, tombstones and coins do give us a good idea about the clothing and hairstyles of the time. Here's a typical outfit for most men, women and children:

A tunic with long or short sleeves and made of varying quality of cloth depending on your wealth.

A cloak (sometimes with a hood) fastened at the shoulder with a bronze brooch.

Leather sandals or **hobnailed shoes.**

The most famous Roman outfit, **the toga**, was actually only worn by a few men, Roman citizens, and perhaps then only on special occasions.

Only for the Ladies

Bronze and bone hairpins for keeping long hair and curls piled up in elaborate hairstyles

Jewellery made of gold, jet and glass

Make-up: chalk to powder the face, red-ochre or red wine dregs for lipstick and blusher, ash for mascara, a mixture of soot and bear fat to blacken eyebrows, face cream for Roman wrinkles – a pot was found in Southwark complete with finger marks!

CHAPTER NINE

GETTING ABOUT

Roman Londoners didn't get about much, in fact you could live all your life without leaving Londinium. But if you were a soldier or in business, then you certainly needed to get from A to B.

ROMAN ROADS

Roads, Roman style, were yet another invention which the Britons could not help being thankful for. Roads, British style, meant dirt tracks worn down through long years of use.

In winter you were lucky if you and your cart got to your destination in one piece. The rutted, churned up and muddy surfaces were a constant hazard, especially when they baked hard in the summer months. Not so Roman roads. They were properly engineered, straight, metalled roads (not made of metal, just a very hard, man-made surface).

In case you ever want to build a road like the Romans did, here's how to do it:

1. First pick two places you want to join up, for example your bedroom and the sweet shop across the park.
2. Dig a deep trench in a straight line between the two. Destroy anything in the way as you go. Don't worry if you have to go through the adventure playground or your teacher's garden.
3. Lay solid foundations of broken stone.
4. Cover that with rammed stone or gravel. Don't forget to give it an arched surface so the water can drain off.
5. Build drainage ditches on either side.
6. Put up a milestone if it's a really long road, longer than a mile.
7. Give your road a name, 'Via' (that means road in Latin) something or other.

But of course, if you were building a road in Roman times you would have been a soldier. The Roman legions were in charge of building the first metalled roads in Britannia. They needed a fast, reliable way of marching from one fort to the next. Later on after the conquest, a network of roads linked up all the new Roman towns. They radiated out of Londinium at the hub. Many modern roads, like Watling Street and the Fosse Way, were laid on top of Roman ones. So next time you're going on a very straight car journey, you never know, you might be on a Roman road.

The first Roman road, the Dover Road, was built by Plautius and his army between the south coast and the future site of Londinium. Don't forget it needed to be strong enough for Claudius and his elephants, let alone constant marching soldiers and their wagons laiden down with supplies.

The main road of Londinium was the Via Decumana which ran east-west across the city. Another went south from this across the river to Southwark and beyond. These are the Roman roads which met in and around Londinium:

1. Watling Street: to Canterbury (Durovernum) and to St Albans (Verulamium)
2. Stane Street: to Chichester (Noviomagus)
3. A road to Silchester (Calleva)
4. Ermine Street: to York (Eburacum)
5. A road to Colchester (Camulodunum)

Foot, Slave or Animal Power

Most people got where they needed to go on foot. But Roman Londoners who had a slave or two to spare, would be carried around in a litter – the name for a chair or bed fastened between two long poles. If they had further to go, then they would go on horse back or in a horse-drawn carriage. Farmers relied on oxen or mules to pull their loads in two or four-wheeled carts. But journeying by road was slow, bumpy and dirty.

SHIP AHOY!

Ships brought the first Roman invaders over to the shores of Britannia. After that, we know that the Romans used ships to import and export goods and supplies by sea and river. How do we know? Have a look at the clues we have so far…

The Clues:

1. A Roman shipwreck was found at Blackfriars. It had a flat bottom, damage on the star-board side and Kentish ragstone was found nearby.
2 At County Hall, near Waterloo, the wreck of a merchant ship was discovered. It had a round bottom and was built in a Mediterranean style.
3. A British-built barge was found at Guy's Hospital.

WHAT THE EXPERTS SAY...

The sailing boat found at Blackfriars had a flat bottom which meant it was good for beaching along the coast to load up with native British goods and also fairly stable. But not stable enough for those reckless river raging sailors! It must have had a violent collision with another vessel on its starboard side and clearly its cargo of Kentish ragstone was tipped overboard. But no remains of any of the sailors were found so let's hope they jumped ship in the nick of time.

The other ship, found at County Hall and with a round bottom, was more a Mediterranean merchant ship that needed to dock at a quayside. A similar one was found in the Thames estuary, wrecked on Pudding Pan Sand, with a cargo of Samian ware (special pottery made in Gaul), bound for London.

Other boats were used for safer journeys transporting food supplies up and down the Thames such as the barge found at Guy's Hospital. The River Thames must have been a busy and dangerous place in Roman times – that's for sure!

An Honest Day's Work in Roman London

Down at the Port

If you were looking for work in Roman London, then the port would have been a good place to start. Archaeologists have found evidence of riverside wharves dating from the late first century through to the late fourth century: at least three hundred years of Roman port activity. Ships docked regularly bringing cargoes from the continent, especially from Gaul and from the Rhineland.

The quayside would have been busy with foreign merchants from all over the empire trading in goods such as olive oil and garum (fish sauce) from southern Spain, wine from the Greek island of Rhodes, fine glass from Italy and Syria, Samian ware pottery from Gaul.

The Amphora –

Another Clever Roman Invention

The grain, wine, olive oil and garum were all stored in long, two handled earthenware jars called amphorae – one appeared in the rotten Roman play in Chapter Six. They were shaped into a point for an ingenious reason. What do you think it was?

A) Their shape made them easy to store.

B) They could be used like a spear for attacking pirates.

C) When they were empty they used to have competitions to see who could spin them round the longest.

Answer: A) *They could be stored upright amongst rocks, packed together in the hold of a merchant ship (up to 6000 at a time) and they could be thrust into the ground easily.*

Buying British

In the early years of the conquest, imports flooded into the new province of Britannia. These kept the Roman army and officials stocked up with food from back home. They were kept happy with luxuries such as olives and wine. So at first, imports far outweighed the exports.

As the province grew and farmers learnt how to grow new crops such as new varieties of wheat (and even grapes) the province didn't need to import so much. In fact, the Romans milked Britannia for all they could get and plenty of British exports found their way to other parts of the empire.

Best of British Exports

Slaves – strong, hard working, honest

Wheat – the finest grade from the fertile soils of Britannia

Oysters – fresh and tasty fruits of the 'Ocean'

Beer – 'worthy of mention' Claudian

Woollen cloth – warm and hard-wearing

Birrus Britannicus – the duffle coat of your dreams, clever hood design keeps out all draughts

Dogs – swift and well-trained for hunting

Lead and tin – a fine combination for the production of pewter: excellent for tableware

Up at the Forum

If you were in business, or in any way connected with the running of the city or the province, then a day's work would very likely mean a trip to the forum. This was the civic centre of Londinium, situated on high ground to the east of the Walbrook stream and north of the bridge and port area.

This huge enclosed courtyard area had a town hall and court of justice (Romans called it the basilica) on the north side and shops and offices on the other sides with room for an open-air market in the middle.

Jobs for the Boys?

Most women of all classes kept their noses to the grindstone too. Wealthy husbands expected their wives to take charge of running the household and bringing up the children.

But many other women may have worked outside the home. For instance, they might have found work in bakeries, mills, fullers (a place where cloth was specially treated) and shops. Wives of traders and craftsmen may have had responsibility for keeping shop or managing an inn or restaurant.

Slave Labour

Life as a slave in Roman London really depended on the type of master you had. There is evidence of a slave market in London. Here wealthy businessmen or their servants would come to buy and sell slaves. Lucky ones would work as a servant in a household or as an administrator in government business. Unlucky ones would be bought to do 'slave labour' on a farm or down the mines. Military officers also needed slaves to help run the forts.

If you were really lucky (and you lived that long) you might be freed after a lengthy period of good service, but not until the great age of thirty (not such a big deal, considering roughly only one in four people lived beyond forty in Roman times). Even luckier still, were the ex-slaves who became imperial freedmen. They weren't at all like slaves, more like senior civil servants. Powerful Polyclitus was one of these. He was sent to Britannia (according to Tacitus) to sort out a dispute in the adminstration. He was so scary that Tacitus called him 'an object of dread'.

MY LIFE AS A SLAVE GIRL IN LONDINIUM BY DILYS

Got up at dawn. Rained in the night again – must tell Victor (he's the new slave, comes from Africa) that hole in the roof needs mending.

Fetched the water as usual from the Walbrook stream. Met Claudia from the Governor's palace. Can't believe it, the emperor's coming to stay and she gets to be the maid for the Emperor's wife – LUCKY BEGGAR! I bet she'll get some good tips!

Next job: stoking the fire in the kitchen stove. Cook was in a rage. Don't blame her. Says she got a real beating last night. The master wasn't pleased with the way the rabbit was cooked so he got his whip out.

Glad to get out of there. Went to buy fruit and veg along the Via Decumana. A new shop's opened selling fish sauce. Don't like the look of it myself. Fancy foreign stuff! Will have to ask Epillicus what you do with it.

When I got back, time for the mistress to get up. Went and helped the others do her hair. What a business! She wanted it like the Governor's wife: all ringlets and plaits. She's off to a birthday party this afternoon. At least we'll get a bit of peace and quiet.

Cook needed help again. She'd calmed down a bit. Still, she made me pluck the thrushes and jackdaws and pull out their entrails – not my favourite job.

Epillicus has bought in a new supply of olive oil. Had to clean out the storeroom all afternoon 'cos he wanted to put it away.

Served at dinnertime. Thank goodness the master liked it today!

Well, just about dead on my feet by the time that was all cleared away.

Wish I was back home in Wales. This city life's not natural. It was tough on the farm but at least I worked for my family.

Fell into bed. Slave labour, that's what I call it.

Talking Your Way to the Top

Business Latin

Whether you liked it or loathed it, Latin was the language of success in Roman London. Anyone who wanted to be anyone knew that speaking and writing Latin was essential. All government business would have been conducted in Latin, even slaves working for the government would have known it.

Anencletus, a slave of the Provincial Council, was one of those slaves who had made good (we know about him because he set up a tombstone to his young wife Claudia discovered in a cemetery near Ludgate). He was clearly educated and held a responsible position. He would have known Latin.

Londinium was a major international port so merchants certainly made it their business to read and write the lingo. Goods were stamped with Latin words and trading documents would have been written in Latin. Wooden tablets with Latin on them have been found preserved in the Walbrook stream.

Latin Adverts

Lucius Julius Senis was an oculist living in Gaul but trying to sell his eye ointment in Londinium. Samian ware cups (a type of pottery only made in Gaul) were stamped with his slogan in Latin:

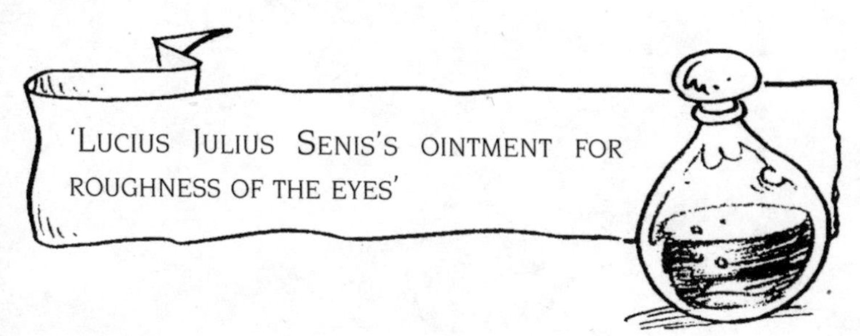

Another merchant based in Antibes in the south of France, advertised his fish sauce (garum) on the amphora it was shipped in:

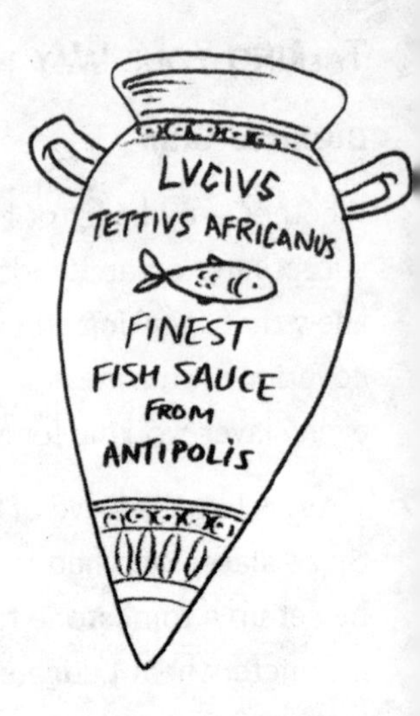

Latin Graffiti

Graffiti even existed in Roman London and it was written in Latin! It was scratched on walls, tiles, pots and writing tablets.

The only problem was, you really couldn't get rid of it once you'd done it. To this day we have some graffiti written by a brickyard worker, complaining about a skiving colleague. Written for ever in the soft clay of a newly made building tile it says (in very bad Latin):

'AUSTALIS HAS BEEN WANDERING OFF ON HIS OWN EVERY DAY FOR A FORTNIGHT.'

Posh Latin

When Agricola was governor of Britannia, he decided to win over the British people by improving their standard of living. He offered a posh Roman education to the sons of the British nobility, including learning Latin. New houses, impressive squares and temples, yes, but the hard work of learning Latin? But Tacitus reports that this bonus went down well (then again, Agricola was his father-in-law):

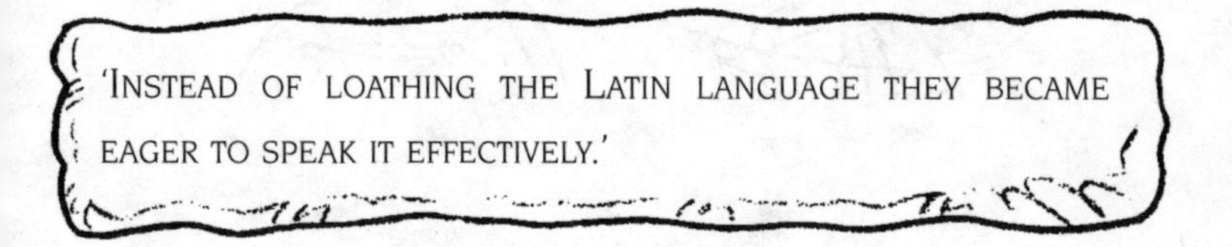

HOW TO GET BY IN LATIN

But for the average Tomius, Dickius or Harrius, it was a matter of learning what you could when you could. Here are some helpful phrases should you ever find yourself in Roman London:

CHAPTER TEN

WHEN NOT IN LONDINIUM

Things began to get more and more messy in the Roman empire from the third century onwards. While Roman generals bickered amongst themselves about who should be emperor, the Goths (barbarian tribes, not teenagers dressed in black) began to attack the eastern frontiers. This was bad news for Britannia. Troops left Britannia to deal with the barbarians. Then raiders from Scotland, Ireland and northern Europe (the Angles and the Saxons) seized their chance to attack vulnerable Britannia.

There was no dramatic exit from Londinium, or from Britannia, for the Romans, no elephants or emperors this time, just a letter. In AD 410, almost four hundred years after the conquest, the Emperor Honorius wrote telling the cities of Britannia that Roman aid had been axed. The Britons were left to defend themselves.

Like a plant that stops being watered, the Roman cities of Britannia now began to wither away and fall into ruins.

In the north, the barbaric peoples were left to wreak wild havoc, according to a British monk called Gildas who described events over a century later:

> 'And so, as the Romans returned home, the loathsome hordes of Scots and Picts eagerly emerged from the coracles that carried them across the gulf of the sea, like dark swarms of worms that emerge from their holes when the sun is high and the weather grows warm. In custom they differed slightly one from another, yet in their single desire for shedding blood they were of one accord.'

In the east, the Anglo-Saxons began to settle in the countryside. The Romans had gone, never to return.

What The Romans Did For Us

But you could say the Romans live on in Britain, even after all these years. The Romans have a lot to do with the way life in Britain is organised today. Politics, culture and learning all owe a lot to the Romans, their ideas and language. Just think, without the Romans there would be no rabbits, wine or peas.

But, of course, the Romans weren't all as fabulous as we'd like to make out. If you could vote for or against the Romans, how would you vote? Here are five good and bad points about the Romans. Read them and then decide how you'd vote.

Good Points:

1 The Romans gave us the names of the months of the year, including changing the start of the year to January, not March – just imagine having Christmas in February…

2. The Romans gave us their language, Latin. Lots of words, names and phrases we use, especially if you're a doctor or a lawyer, are from the Latin language. Fancy names like Marcus, Julian, Claudia and Olivia are all Roman names.

3. We still use Roman numerals. Can you picture Big Ben without its Roman clockface?

4. Roman roads aren't bendy but dead straight so they stop you feeling car sick.

5. Mosaics, like the ones at the swimming pool or in your shower, were invented by the Romans.

Bad Points:

1. If your mum has to force you to eat peas, carrots, cucumbers or cabbage, then blame it on the Romans who introduced them to Britain.

2. You might find spelling words like aquarium really difficult. It's based on a Latin word.

3. Your older brother or sister think they can boss you about like a slave because the Romans did.

4. Some teachers still think it's fashionable to wear Roman style sandals and duffle coats.

5. The first schools in London were set up by the Romans. Yes, it's the Romans' fault you have to go to school.

How would you judge them?

Places to Visit

You need to go armed with a copy of the Ordnance Survey map of Londinium and a healthy imagination. London is built on centuries of rubbish so the street level of Roman London would have been five or six metres lower.

•

London Stone, possibly the central milestone of the province and originally located on the south side of Cannon Street, is now preserved in the wall of the Overseas Chinese Banking Corporation, 111 Cannon Street, EC4 5AS.

•

The ground plan of the **Temple of Mithras** can be seen in Queen Victoria Street, on the courtyard in front of the Sumitomo Bank/Legal & General Building, London EC4. It was moved and reconstructed from original building material at Temple Court, 11 Queen Victoria Street. EC4.

•

The site of the **Huggin Hill Baths** is marked by some terraced gardens at Huggin Hill, EC4.

•

The Roman Bath, 5 Strand Lane, WC2R 2NA was restored in the seventeenth century and believed by some to be Roman. Visible all year round from the pathway, approach via Surrey Street.

Parts of the Roman London Wall can be seen at the **Museum of London**, 150 London Wall, EC2Y 5HN, and also a part rebuilt in medieval times at **Tower Hill**, EC3. There's also a statue 'believed to be of the Roman Emperor Trajan' outside Tower Hill tube station.

•

St Peter upon Cornhill, Cornhill, EC3V 9DS is reputedly the oldest place of Christian worship in London, having being founded on the site of the Roman basilica by Lucius, the first Christian ruler of Britain, in AD 179.

•

St Magnus the Martyr, Lower Thames Street, EC3R 6DN, once stood at the head of medieval London Bridge. The remains of a Roman wharf stand in the churchyard.

•

The Walbrook Stream no longer exists but you can walk along the street called Walbrook, EC4, and follow where the stream once flowed.

•

The Roman London Bridge would have crossed the Thames at the bottom of Fish Street Hill, EC3, just beside London Bridge.

•

Cannon Street Station, Cannon Street, EC4 marks the spot where the Roman Governor's palace once stood.

•

Boudicca is said to be buried underneath platform 9 of **King's Cross Station**, NI. If you want to see her statue, it is by **Westminster Bridge**, Westminster, SW1 opposite Big Ben.

The Museum of London, at 150 London Wall, London, EC2Y 5HN has re-creations of Roman workshops, house interiors and displays of many Roman artefacts including a Roman horse and a leather bikini. It is also home to the Spitalfields Roman. www.museumoflondon.org.uk. Tel 020 7600 3699.

•

The British Museum, Great Russell Street, Bloomsbury, WC1B 3DG, has a fine display of objects from Roman London including a mosaic from the Bank of England and another from Leadenhall Street as well as the tomb of Gaius Julius Alpinus Classicianus, the procurator sent to calm things down after Boudicca's rebellion. www.thebritishmuseum.ac.uk. Tel 020 7636 1555.

•

The Museum in Docklands, No. 1 Warehouse, West India Quay, Hertsmere Road E14 4A, tells the story of the Roman port. www.museumindocklands.org.uk. Tel 0870 444 3857.

Out of Town

If you're really interested, **Fishbourne Roman Palace**, Salthill Road, Fishbourne, West Sussex PO19 3QR, two miles from Chichester is worth a visit. www.sussexpast.co.uk. Tel 01243 785 859.

•

At **Colchester Castle Museum**, 14 Ryegate Road Colchester, Essex CO1 1YG, you can see the foundations of the Roman temple of Claudius. www.colchestermuseums.org.uk. Tel 01206 282 927.

•

The town of St Albans is definitely worth a trip too for the **Verulamium Museum and Roman Town**, St Michael's Street St Albans Hertfordshire AL3 4SW, as well as the rare example of a true Roman theatre in Britain. www.stalbansmuseums.org.uk. Tel 01727 751 810.

OTHER BOOKS FROM WATLING STREET YOU'LL LOVE IN THIS SERIES:

The Timetraveller's Guide to Saxon and Viking London

by Joshua Doder

Journey back to London when it was home to some of the funniest names and the foulest food in English history!

ISBN 1-904153-07-0

•

The Timetraveller's Guide to Medieval London

by Christine Kidney

Scratch, sniff and itch your way around the capital during its smelliest period in history.

ISBN1-904153-08-9

•

The Timetraveller's Guide to Shakespeare's London

by Joshua Doder

William Shakespeare is our greatest writer; read all about him, his plays and the big bad city he lived and worked in.

ISBN 1-904153-10-0

•

The Timetraveller's Guide to Tudor London

by Natasha Narayan

See the terrible tyrants, cruel queens, conmen and cutpurses in Tudor London's dark, dingy and all too dangerous streets.

ISBN 1-904153-09-7

•

The Timetraveller's Guide to Victorian London

by Natasha Narayan

Get robbed and meet the snobs on a tour of Queen Vic's top town.

ISBN 1-904153-11-9